CUTTING-EDGE CAREERS™

CAREERS IN
COMPUTER
GAMING

Matthew Robinson

ROSEN
PUBLISHING®

New York

Published in 2007 by The Rosen Publishing Group, Inc.
29 East 21st Street, New York, NY 10010

Library of Congress Cataloging-in-Publication Data

Robinson, Matthew.
Careers in computer gaming/Matthew Robinson.
    p. cm. — (Cutting-edge careers)
Includes bibliographical references and index.
ISBN-13: 978-1-4042-0958-9
ISBN-10: 1-4042-0958-1 (library binding)
1. Computer games—Programming—Vocational guidance. 2. Video games—Design—Vocational guidance. I. Title.

QA76.76.C672R634 2006
794.8'1526023—dc22
2006023274

Manufactured in the United States of America

CONTENTS

INTRODUCTION

[T] he first interactive computer game was created in 1961 by an MIT student named Steve Russell. The game was called *Spacewar*, and it was coded by Russell on a minicomputer known as the Digital PDP-1 (or Programmed Data Processor-1). Unlike most computers today, the Digital PDP-1 did not have an internal hard drive. Instead, it received all of its information from "paper tape," a long, thin strip of paper filled with tiny holes.

In 1971, Nolan Bushnell (who would later go on to create the Atari company) released *Computer Space*, the first coin-operated computer arcade game the world had ever seen. Like *Spacewar*, *Computer Space* involved a small spaceship struggling to survive in a hostile outer-space environment. However, the game was commercially unsuccessful as many people considered it to be too complicated.

The year 1972 saw the world's first console gaming system, the Odyssey. It was designed by Ralph Baer and manufactured by Magnavox. The black-and-white visuals produced by the console were augmented by colorful plastic overlays designed to stick onto one's television screen in order to simulate color graphics. The games on the Magnavox Odyssey (*Tennis*, *Ski*, and *Simon Says*, to name a few) ran completely silent, employing no audio track or sound effects.

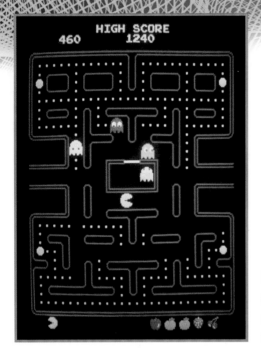

HIGH SCORE
460   1240

Commercially successful arcade games such as *Pac-Man (shown here)* and *Pong* helped pave the way for the worldwide popularity of video games.

The aptly named *Pong*, also released in 1972, derived its name in part from the game Ping-Pong and in part from the sound effects found in the game. *Pong* is considered the world's first commercially successful coin-operated computer arcade game. In 1976, Atari released the home console version of *Pong*. The console system came with two paddle-shaped controllers and played only one game: *Pong*.

In 1986, Nintendo, a Japanese company, released the Nintendo Entertainment System (NES) worldwide. The system went on to sell more than half a million units in its first two months. Nintendo's home console system boasted 8-bit graphics and a cast of soon-to-be iconic characters such as Mario, Luigi, Link, Zelda, and Donkey Kong. The NES was a major turning point in the history of video games, signaling to the world that video games could be commercially successful and culturally significant.

The Video Game Industry Today

Today, the video game business is a $10 billion-a-year industry. With the sales of video game software and home and portable consoles, the industry takes in a larger annual income than do the motion picture, music, and publishing industries combined.

The old video games were in black and white, could display only a few polygons on the screen at a time, and used "blips" and "bloops" as the entire soundtrack. Today, video games can be found in high definition (HD), displaying millions of colors and emitting stereo surround sound.

Now is a great time to start thinking about a career in computer gaming. Along with the Internet came the birth of online gaming, which is the future of video games. More than ever, gamers are uniting over high-speed Internet connections to compete in epic battles, help each other solve puzzles, form online communities, and make new friends. Whether the future of gaming lies in massive multiplayer online role-playing games (MMORPGs), motion sensor controllers, or even virtual reality video games, the computer gaming industry is at the forefront of exciting careers in cutting-edge technology.

What It Takes to Work in the Video Game Industry

While playing video games on a console, online, or at a coin-op arcade can be a lot of fun, the process of actually making a great video game requires passion, experience, and dedication. So how do you know if a career in computer gaming is right for you?

Whether you're a casual or a hard-core gamer, the first prerequisite for a career in the video game industry is a passion for gaming. You don't have to be a fan of all video game genres. As long as you truly enjoy playing games, talking about games, and thinking about games,

Today's video game industry employs the latest technologies, including high-definition (HD) graphics, movie-quality surround sound audio, and online multiplayer capabilities.

you already have the foundation for what it takes to make it in the video game industry.

You're also going to need an understanding of the industry's cutting-edge technologies. Technology is one of the most—if not *the most*—important elements of the video game industry. An understanding of cutting-edge technologies will help you create better games that push the industry to new heights.

The best way to prepare for a career in computer gaming is to consider the many different career options available to you in the field. Which career type appeals to you most? Which one would best utilize your natural talents? Which one would you enjoy the most?

After all, a fully fledged video game takes dozens, if not hundreds, of people to bring it to life. No one person can create an entire game on his or her own. In fact, anyone looking for a job in computer gaming needs to have experience (and in some cases even *expertise*) in at least one particular field. Understanding the many career options available to you in the world of computer gaming will help you in choosing the career path best suited to you.

CHAPTER 1

The World of Computer Gaming

The two main divisions involved in creating a video game are the development and production teams. The functions of the development team are to design the game and move it from an initial concept into a fully realized, playable, and entertaining video game. Development jobs are usually more creative and artistic than production jobs. The role of the production team is to oversee the development team, make sure the game develops into an entertaining product, and eventually market and sell the game to the largest buying audience possible. In most cases, the production team is responsible for the financial funding behind the game. Often, but not always, production jobs are oriented more toward people with managerial and business-related skills.

Whether creating video games on the development team or the production team, a career in computer gaming can be a fun, exciting, and rewarding experience.

Sometimes it is the production team that has an idea for a video game and then searches for the right development team to bring it to life. At other times, it is the developers who pitch an original idea to different production companies in hopes of finding the right company to turn their idea into a reality. Regardless of who comes up with the initial idea, every video game needs to have one team in charge of the actual building and design of the game and one team in charge of overseeing, financing, and marketing the game.

While the production and development teams usually work separately, many video game companies find it easier to do both jobs themselves. The way a video game company does this is by having its own in-house development team. In other words, the people responsible for designing and building the game work exclusively for that production company and develop games only for it. This is referred to as internal development. If a development team doesn't work exclusively for one video game company, then it is referred to as external development.

Whether you're interested in working on the production side or the development side (or both), understanding the differences between the two is an integral part of understanding how video games are made.

The Initial Concept

The first step in the creation of a video game is coming up with the initial concept. There are two different types of initial concepts: original IP (intellectual property) and licensed property. An original IP is a brand-new idea that is not based on any other previously created entertainment medium, like a movie or a comic book. An original IP usually involves the creation of brand-new characters, environment, and/or storyline. Because the characters, name, and storyline are unfamiliar to the public prior to the game's release, an original IP is a very risky type of game to produce, both from a production and development standpoint. A good example of a successful original IP is *Halo*. Made for Microsoft's Xbox console, *Halo* has become a best seller with an iconic main character.

Creating a video game based on an already well-known license is a much less risky endeavor. By taking a popular film, comic book, or character and paying for the rights to use that license as the basis for a video game, you are guaranteed to have a built-in audience that knows what to expect in your game. A good example of a licensed property is any of the many Harry Potter games currently available for most PC and home console systems.

Andy Kerridge *(left)* and Simon Phipps, the game designers behind *Harry Potter and the Prisoner of Azkaban*, turned the popular book by J. K. Rowling into an interactive video game experience.

Preproduction

Preproduction is the stage during which the production team and development team expand upon their initial concept, begin to get a visual and technical feel for the game, and prepare financially and managerially for the task of creating the game. A large part of preproduction is creating a design document. The design document is created by the game designer and the art design department to show examples of how they believe the video game should look. It gives the production team an idea of the game's visual style and art direction, and helps everyone on the development team gain a singular vision of the game at hand.

On the technical side of things, preproduction allows the programmers a chance to play around with the video game engine that will run the actual game. If the game is going to have some exciting new lighting effects or a new physics engine, preproduction is where the programmers will have an opportunity to show an early example of how they plan on actually pulling off these new game-specific technologies.

Production

Production involves the actual design and creation of the video game. During this stage, the specifications outlined in the design document are turned into moving, controllable characters, and the programmers turn computer codes into interactive entertainment software. Production can last anywhere from a few months to a few years, depending on the size and budget of the video game. During production, hours are long, stress is high, and creativity and managerial skills are put to the test.

Testing
Testing is an extremely important part of the production process. It is so important that a large portion of the production schedule is based upon testing deadlines known as alpha and beta.

Testing begins as soon as there is a playable version or portion of the video game. Testers are brought in to play the video game and search for bugs (problems in the code that cause the game to act differently than intended). The testers then report the bugs to the programmers, who then do their best to repair them. Because of the large amount of written code in a modern video game and the complicated nature of game designing in general, it can take months—if not years—for a video game to be considered bug-free and ready to ship out to buyers.

In order to structure the testing process, there are two main testing deadlines. These are the major milestones in the game's production that let everyone know how far along they are in the process.

At the alpha stage, a playable version of the entire game is tested. All of the artwork might not be implemented, and the sound effects and score might be missing. Even a few characters might be out of place. The term "alpha" also refers to this rough draft of the entire game.

At the beta stage, a much more polished version of the game is tested. All of the artwork is in the game, as well as all of the sound effects and music. For all intents and purposes, this is the game as it is meant to be seen and played. At this point in the process, the game is often released to a small section of the public to help the development team and the testers search out any remaining bugs.

Once the game has spent some time in beta, and everyone on both the development and production teams agrees that the game is ready to be shipped, it is sent off to a distributor (a company whose job is to get the video games into the actual stores) and then sold to the general public.

The Different Genres of Video Games

Another aspect to consider in thinking about potential career paths in the video game industry is that of genre. A video game genre is simply a specific type of video game. For example, sports games, first-person shooters (FPS), and role-playing games are all different genres of video games. Because the development and production processes may vary depending on the genre, many development and production teams work exclusively in one or two video game genres. It is important to consider what genres you enjoy and believe your passions and talents would be most compatible with.

Sports

Whether they're based on a national pastime such as baseball or football, or on a more free-form extreme sport, like snowboarding or skateboarding, sports games give players an opportunity to live their athletic fantasies. Players either take the role of their favorite teams or players, or create their own teams or players to beat the competition with their fast reflexes and strategic playmaking. *John Madden Football* and *Tony Hawk Pro Skater* are examples of popular sports video games.

Racing and Vehicle Simulation Games

Racing games focus on the simulation of getting behind the wheel of vehicles most of us will never have the opportunity to drive or fly. Whether you like wheeling around a wacky track in a go-cart or racing a photo-realistic Formula 1 car, racing games are tailor-made for the speed demon in all of us. Vehicle simulation games include flight simulators and all other vehicle simulation programs that focus heavily on realism and accuracy. Popular games in this genre include *Gran Turismo*, *Mario Kart*, and *Microsoft Flight Simulator*.

Action/Adventure

Starting with games such as *Pong* and *Pac-Man*, the action/adventure genre was the first genre in the video game industry and is still the most popular. The action/adventure genre contains many subgenres, but all of them have one thing in common—fast-paced excitement that requires quick reflexes and precise control of the main character. One of the most popular subgenres of action/adventure is the first-person shooter (or FPS), like *Halo*. The FPS puts you behind the eyes of the main character. Usually, all you can see is your character's hands and feet, and you are immersed in a fully 3-D world in which you are the main character. Other subgenres include the third-person

Wrestling video games and other popular titles in the sports genre give players a chance to live out their athletic fantasies.

shooter (for example, *Resident Evil*), fighting games *(Street Fighter II)*, adventure games *(The Legend of Zelda: the Wind Waker)*, and platform games *(Super Mario Bros)*.

Simulation

With the immense popularity of games such as *The Sims* (the best-selling computer game of all time), the simulation genre has become one of the most important and financially successful genres in the video game industry. Simulation games give you an opportunity to manage the day-to-day functions of entire cities, worlds, families, theme parks, or almost anything else you can imagine being in charge of. For example, in *The Sims*, the player is given control of a simulated human being and tasked with building that character a home, finding him or her a career, and eventually starting a family. For people who love playing in a giant virtual sandbox in which the ability to destroy or create at will is in their hands, simulation games offer a unique, immersive experience. *Rollercoaster Tycoon* is another popular simulation game.

Role-Playing Games

Also referred to as RPGs, role-playing games take their inspiration from dice-based games such as Dungeons & Dragons. RPGs often involve "leveling up" your character in order to progress in the game by completing certain missions or tasks. Most RPGs still work on the dice-based gameplay mechanics, only the rolling of the dice happens behind the scenes and often in real-time. For example, in your average fantasy-based RPG, if your level 9 Warrior attacks a level 9 Troll, the RPG engine is usually "rolling the dice" behind the scenes to see how much damage your player will take and/or receive. RPGs are great for gamers who love long-lasting, often nonlinear, character-management gameplay experiences that borrow heavily from the fantasy worlds of swords and sorcery. *Final Fantasy* is a fine example of an RPG.

John Riccitiello, former president of game publisher Electronic Arts, poses next to *The Sims*, the popular simulation game that puts the gamer in charge of a simulated household.

Strategy and Real-Time Strategy

The strategy and real-time strategy genre usually focuses on war simulation and strategy. Often pitting one army against another in an expansive environment and giving each side only a limited number of assets and weapons, strategy and real-time strategy (often abbreviated as RTS) games can easily take on a very chesslike feel. Putting a game in real time means that, unlike chess, the game is not turn-based. Both sides of the battle are working to defeat the other in whichever time frame they see fit. *Warcraft, Command & Conquer* is an example of a strategy game.

Massive Multiplayer Online Role-Playing Games (MMORPGs)

A relatively new genre, the MMORPG has quickly become one of the most popular and financially lucrative genres being created today. Unlike traditional role-playing games, the MMORPG requires an Internet connection (usually broadband) and cannot be played off-line. In an MMORPG, you play against other players scattered across the globe, as well as computer-controlled characters found within the game. The game takes place in a "persistent world," meaning that even when you log off your computer, the video game world continues to exist. MMORPGs rarely have an ending and can be played for hundreds of hours without repeating a single mission or task. Creators of MMORPGs have to constantly keep an eye on their virtual world, making sure things are working smoothly, adding additional content to keep players satisfied, and releasing "patches" to fix bugs or make changes. This is why most MMORPGs charge their customers a monthly fee in addition to the cost of the software. Popular MMORPGs include *Everquest* and *World of Warcraft*.

Puzzle Games

A simple yet extremely popular genre, puzzle games are built to be played in short spurts and usually involve either solving a series of puzzles or setting a high score. *Tetris*, generally considered to be the world's most popular and widely played video game, set the standard early on in the 1980s for the puzzle game genre.

Unclassifiable

While the vast majority of games released today can be placed into one of the previously described genres, occasionally a game is released that tries something completely different and therefore doesn't fit into any known video game genre. Dancing and karaoke games, or even top-selling games such as *Myst* often live on as genres unto themselves. When thinking of new game ideas or possible changes you would make to the video game industry, don't get boxed in by the concept of genre. After all, you could be the one to create a brand-new video game genre. Your idea could go on to become a cultural phenomenon that changes the video game industry forever.

Now that you have a general understanding of the video game industry and how a video game comes to life, it's time to examine the many different jobs involved in video game creation.

CHAPTER 2

Programming, Art Design, and Audio Design

The programmer, art designer, and music designer are the three professionals who are most involved in the actual building of a video game. They are members of the development team. The programmer writes the code that tells the game software what to do, the artist creates the visual style and animations that bring the game to life, and the music designer composes sound effects and dramatic music to transform the game into a blockbuster experience.

Programming

Programmers create the software on which the art, animation, script, music, and sound effects run. Without the programmer,

A video game programmer must have extensive experience with the latest computer technologies, a great attention to detail, and a passion for video games.

a video game would simply be a collection of unanimated characters and backgrounds, a script, and a few tracks of music. The software and the coding behind the software are what bring the game to life. They inform each little pixel on screen what task to perform and how to perform it.

In the field of video game programming, there are many subcategories in which to specialize. In fact, today's game development teams usually have a few different types of programmers under the same roof who all do very specific jobs. For example, graphics programmer, game physics programmer, artificial intelligence (AI) programmer, and network and server programmer are a few of the more well-known programmer specializations.

Hours involved: Typical forty-hour workweek, but can often turn into a sixty- to eighty-hour workweek during game production.
Work environment: Almost always in front of a computer.
Salary: Starting salary around $50,000; more experienced programmers can make $115,000 and up.

Educational Qualifications

Programming is not something you can learn while on the job. It can take years, if not decades, to master. Whether you're self-taught or school-taught, you'll spend many hours in front of a computer screen or with your nose buried behind a book before you'll be able to find work as a programmer with a major game developer.

While not all game production and development teams demand that their applicants have a programming-related college degree, taking classes in programming can be a great way to get your hands on a variety of different computers and make industry connections that can help you down the road. A degree in computer sciences is highly recommended for anyone interested in becoming a programmer. Today, many large colleges and universities (and even some of the smaller ones) offer courses in computer science and computer programming. There are even trade schools nationwide that specialize in video game programming.

Skills Set

Designing software, writing code, and debugging are the three main skills all programmers must master. In order to accomplish these tasks, they need to be proficient in a handful of different computer programs and languages.

A programmer's greatest asset is his or her understanding of the software programs and languages used by the industry today to build and design video games. A computer language is the way in which the programmer communicates with the computer to tell the software what to do. This language is written as code. The industrywide standard computer language is called C++. A programmer who isn't familiar with C++ will not be able to write or communicate with the software used today by the video game industry.

The following are a few of the programs most widely used today by programmers and are worth having a general understanding of for anyone interested in a career in video game programming.

C++: Most commonly and widely used code language for writing video game software.

DirectX or OpenGL: Commonly referred to as API (short for application programming interface), these programs allow the programmer to instruct the software on how to interface with the hardware.

CodeWarrior: Used for safely writing code and quickly tracking down bugs.

Java, Macromedia Flash: Used mostly for Web-based games and graphics, but still important tools for any programmer to know.

Photoshop, Maya, and 3D Studio Max: Allow 2-D and 3-D design and animation. Although most often used by art designers and animators, these programs are still very important for programmers to have an understanding of as well.

Personal Traits

If you're the type of person who loves taking computers apart and putting them back together, thinks of yourself as a "math person," and doesn't mind spending hours staring at lines of code on a computer screen, then programming might be the career path for you.

For the most part, programmers must be logical, methodical, and extremely patient. Sifting though thousands of lines of code in order to find a small bug that is preventing the entire game from running can be a tedious job that requires a careful, organized mind.

How to Get Your Foot in the Door

The best way to get a start as a programmer is to begin writing simple programs on your home computer. Picking up a beginner's guide to C++ is the best way to start honing your code-writing skills. Create a few small programs, become familiar with the code-writing process, and keep challenging yourself.

Becoming involved with your school's computer lab or getting a summer internship at a local game production or development company can be a great way to get some hands-on experience and mentoring.

Art Design

The majority of people involved in creating a video game can be found in the art and animation departments. This is because the most amount of time, energy, and (usually) budget goes toward creating the visual look of the game.

The art designers take the code written by the programmers and turn it into a visual world the players can interact with. From the lush background of an environment to the weapons and objects scattered through a level to the expressions in the characters' faces, every visual you see in a video game was drawn and created by the artists and animators on the art design team.

Being an artist or an animator is a very creative job. Although an art designer takes most of his or her instruction from the lead game designer on what exactly should be drawn, he or she also has a great deal of creative input on how the game ends up looking and is often consulted for new ideas and designs.

3-D animation software (like the one pictured here) is just one of the many important tools used by art designers to create the visual look of today's video games.

Hours involved: Typical forty-hour workweek, but can often turn into a sixty- to eighty-hour workweek during game production.

Work environment: Either out in the real world getting inspiration or back at the office drawing or animating on a computer.

Salary: Starting salary around $40,000; more experienced art designers can make $80,000 and up.

Educational Qualifications

A four-year degree in art is recommended for anyone hoping to find a career in video game art design. Being trained as a visual artist, not just a video game artist, is an extremely important part of being a video game art designer. An artist working for a video game development company will be expected to be comfortable with all forms of visual art, whether drawing on paper or on computer drawing tablets.

Many colleges and universities today have begun to offer art programs tailored to those interested in video game art and animation. There are even trade schools nationwide that specialize in video game art design.

Skills Set

First and foremost, you must be a visual artist. You must be able to sketch, draw, and paint a wide range of characters, environments, and objects. If you consider yourself an artist or feel you've always had a natural talent for drawing, sketching, painting, or sculpting, then you might be perfect for a career as an art designer.

Being comfortable with math, computers, and even a little programming are important skills as well for anyone interested in video game art design.

The following software programs are a few of the most important tools available to the video game artist today.

Art designers create the many character animations needed to bring a video game character to life. Pictured here are the various stages of movement for the video game *Rayman*.

Maya and 3D Studio Max: Two of the most widely used 3-D modeling and animation programs.

Photoshop: The industry standard for 2-D visuals and texturing.

Personal Traits

An attention to detail is a very important personal trait for the video game art designer. Strong communication skills are helpful, since artists will often need to describe the designs they see in their heads before being tasked with implementing them. Good people skills are also important, as art designers work very closely with programmers. The artists need to make sure that the visuals they are creating will work with the software being designed by the programmers, and vice versa.

How to Get Your Foot in the Door

Keeping a sketch book with you and sketching as often as possible is a great way to hone your skills as an artist. Try drawing a different object you see every day.

The first thing a video game employer will look at is your portfolio, which is a collection of your artwork, so start coming up with eye-catching, original designs. Entering your artwork in local competitions or art fairs is a great way to get your work seen by others and a great way to get constructive feedback.

A summer apprenticeship or internship at a video game production company can lead to important job connections down the road.

Audio Design

The first video game audio designers had little more than a sequence of "blips" and "bloops" to help them bring the sounds in their games to life. Today, video game audio designers employ a full range of motion picture–quality music and sound design tools. Whether creating sound effects on a foley stage (a sound stage specially designed to record sound effects) or conducting a score with the London Philharmonic, the video game audio designer has an exciting, cutting-edge job.

The audio designers are responsible for the game's sound effects, the voices heard within the game, and the game's score (or music). On smaller games, all of the audio work may be done on a handful of computers with a series of synthesizers, a few musicians, and a music recording program such as Pro Tools. On larger games, the audio designers might be split up into different groups, each one assigned to different tasks, like researching sound effects, writing the score, recording the dialogue, and many other audio-related tasks.

Video game audio designers use many of the same professionals, techniques, and recording technologies used by the motion picture industry to create the audio for big-budget summer blockbusters.

Hours involved: Typical forty-hour workweek, but can often turn into a sixty- to eighty- hour workweek during game production.
Work environment: Capturing sounds out in the real world or recording them in a music studio.
Salary: Starting salary around $60,000; more experienced audio designers can make $90,000 and up.

Educational Qualifications

As the field of video game audio design is relatively new, not many colleges or universities offer specific degrees or courses in the subject.

A potential employer at a video game company will be interested in your technical experience in music recording, as well as your musical creativity.

Many colleges, universities, and trade schools offer courses in audio engineering. These courses provide a quick way to learn the technical side of the business. Because a good amount of video game audio is created on a synthesizer, a strong background in piano is highly recommended, too.

Skills Set

Whether you're interested in being a musician or an audio engineer, or both, video game audio design might be the perfect career choice for you. The technical and creative branches of audio design cross paths often, but you don't have to be a master in both to make a name for yourself in the industry.

If musicianship is your strongest skill, whether playing an instrument or piano or composing music, then you may be better suited for composing scores. If working behind the scenes seems more in line with your natural talents, then a career in video game sound recording, mixing, and editing might be in your future. Perhaps you have a knack for remembering or recreating sounds found in the real world. If so, a career in sound effects recording and engineering might be perfect for you.

The following are the software tools most widely used by video game audio designers today.

> Pro Tools: Known as a digital audio workstation (or DAW), Pro Tools is the industry standard for recording, editing, and mixing all types of audio tracks and files.
>
> Cubase: Similar to Pro Tools, Cubase began primarily as a MIDI (musical instrument digital interface) recording tool, meaning that it was able to re-create the sounds of instruments digitally (usually with a synthesizer).

A thorough understanding of music theory and musicianship, a familiarity with cutting-edge computer technologies, and a passion for video games are the necessary traits of a video game audio designer.

Personal Traits

Audio designers spend a lot of their time recording sounds found in the real world and re-creating or tweaking them back in the recording studio or on their computers. This is why the most important trait of an audio designer is the ability to listen. Become familiar with different sounds found in the real world and store them away in your mind for the day you might need to re-create them again.

A passion for music and sound and a love for writing, recording, or playing different types of music are musts for anyone interested in a career in audio design.

How to Get Your Foot in the Door

Becoming proficient with an instrument is the first step toward a career in audio design. Having an understanding of at least one type of instrument will give you a great foundation in music theory. Joining the school band can also be a great way to learn how different instruments are played and how different types of music are composed.

A summer internship at a video game development company or a recording studio can be a great way to get some hands-on experience in the industry and make some great connections as well.

Cutting Edge Careers
Cutting Edge Careers
Careers
Cutting Edge Careers

Game Design and Writing

Now that we've covered the professions involved in the actual building of a video game, it's time to take a look at the men and women responsible for the ideas behind the games—the game designers and writers. These two professions are found on the development team. If you have a love for storytelling and a knack for bringing ideas to life, then a career in game design or writing might be perfect for you.

Game Design

The game designer is to the video game what the movie director is to the movie. The game designer is often, but not always,

The video game designer must be able to succinctly communicate his or her vision of the video game to every member of the development and production teams.

the person who comes up with the initial idea for the game. It is the game designer who must have a vision of how the game will look, feel, and play, and then make sure everyone else working on the video game shares that vision.

Whether explaining to the physics programmer how the main character's jump move should feel to the player, or describing what an end-level boss should look like to an art designer, or even playing video games in the name of research, the game designer is the jack-of-all-trades who is involved in every aspect of video game creation.

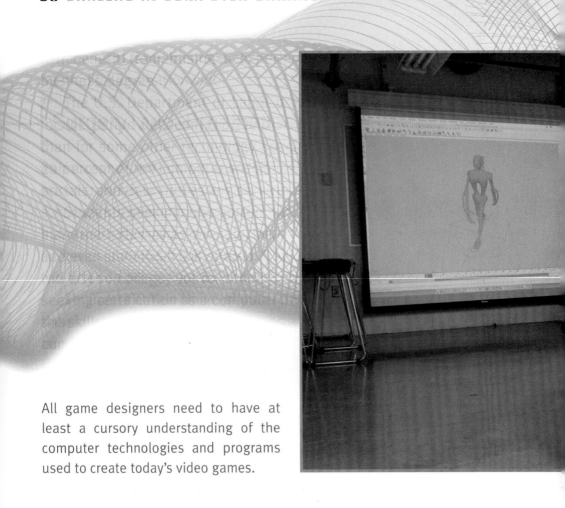

All game designers need to have at least a cursory understanding of the computer technologies and programs used to create today's video games.

Hours involved: Typical forty-hour workweek, but can often turn into a sixty- to eighty- hour workweek during game production.

Work environment: Studying video games in various places and overseeing the development team in the office.

Salary: Starting salary around $40,000; more experienced game designers can make $75,000 and up.

Educational Qualifications

Because the game designer must have an understanding of nearly every aspect of video game production, there is no standard set of qualifications most employers look for. For the same reason, being a

game designer is rarely anyone's first job in the video game industry. Many game designers start out as testers or even programmers.

A large part of a game designer's job is coming up with entertaining video game concepts and then fleshing them out into fully realized characters and storylines. Therefore, a background in writing and literature would be extremely helpful.

Some trade schools offer classes in game design and level building. However, because a game designer must have experience in so many different aspects of the game-making process, actual experience in the gaming industry may be more valuable to a potential employer.

Skills Set

A solid sense of story, an understanding of how video games are created, a vast knowledge of video games, and a vision for the future of the industry are important skills all game designers should have. A game designer needs to be able to quickly understand a technical problem being faced by a programmer or the hardware requirements involved in the visual design of a game. Therefore, it is important that he or she has at least a cursory understanding of all of the programs being used in the video game industry today.

Personal Traits

Leadership and people skills are a must for this position. You've got to be able to communicate your thoughts articulately and patiently to a large group of people who may understand and visualize concepts differently than you do.

Game design can be a long, arduous task, but its reward is the excitement of watching a video game grow from a basic idea to a well-made product being shipped to gamers all over the world.

How to Get Your Foot in the Door

Getting a job as a game designer is based solely on experience in the video game industry. The best way in is to start as a video game tester or an intern at a video game company and slowly work your way up, gaining experience in as many different video game fields as possible.

Writing

Just as every movie starts with a script, so does every video game. Video games have always had writers, but in the past few years,

Because today's video games tell longer stories with more dialogue and written text, the job of the video game writer is more important than ever to the video game industry.

video game writers have had a lot more writing to do. It's only in the past few generations of video game consoles and PC processors that video games have been able to store hundreds, if not thousands, of lines of recorded dialogue. Because games can now hold such a large amount of data, writers have to write longer scripts with more characters, dialogue, and plot twists. In fact, today's video game scripts can run anywhere from 300 to 600 pages long. Compare that to the average feature-length movie script of around 120 pages.

Whether it's writing pitches for original IPs or being hired by a development team to write the script for a game in preproduction, the job of the video game writer is an important and exciting one in the industry.

Hours involved: Typical forty-hour workweek, but can often turn into a sixty- to eighty-hour workweek during game production.

Work environment: Video game writers work both from home and in the development office. They spend the majority of their time reading books or working on their computers.

Salary: Starting salary around $60,000; more experienced writers can make $150,000 and up.

Educational Qualifications

Most video game production companies look for a bachelor's degree in English from their prospective writers. Many video game writers today got their start in Hollywood, writing scripts for the motion picture industry. Taking classes on screenwriting or having some experience in the entertainment industry is a big plus.

Skills Set

You've got to be a proficient writer of prose, both fiction and nonfiction. Writers in the video game industry will be expected to write technical manuals, in-game text, entire game scripts, and character dialogue, just to name a few examples. A writer's technical tools are as simple as a word processor or script writing program.

Microsoft Word: The industry standard word processor.
Final Draft: Script writing program.

Personal Traits

You've got to be a fast writer, comfortable with the written word, and highly creative. Writers have to be able to keep a cool head under hard-to-meet deadlines and high-pressure turnarounds. People skills are important as well, since writers spend a lot of time pitching or explaining their ideas to others.

How to Get Your Foot in the Door

Get as much writing experience as possible. Whether you're writing for your school newspaper or writing articles for gaming magazines, do whatever you can to get some experience under your belt.

An internship with a video game production company or a video game industry magazine can be a great way to learn more about writing and make some connections along the way.

CHAPTER 4

Game Testing and Marketing

Before a video game can be placed on store shelves, it has to be adequately tested and marketed. This is where the professions of game tester and marketer come into play. The game tester is usually on the development team, although some production teams hire their own game testers as the game gets closer to its release date. Game testers look for bugs within the software to make sure that the game runs without a hitch. The marketer uses advertising to alert the public as much as possible about the video game before it goes on sale. Marketers are on the production side. If you've got patience, diligence, and a love for video games, one of these two professions might suit you well.

Video game testing can be a fun, exciting way to play the latest video games before they hit the stores. However, being a game tester takes a lot of patience and diligence.

Game Testing

Put simply, testers are paid to play video games all day long. Yet the life of a tester isn't all fun and games. Testers play video games with only one goal in mind: to find as many bugs in the software as possible.

The work of a tester usually involves playing different builds (versions) of the same video game for months on end, attempting to cause the game to "glitch," "crash," "freeze," or show any other sign that lets the tester know he or she has found a bug. The tester then tries to re-create the bug, usually videotaping the bug in action on the screen with a DVD or VCR deck attached to the television. Every re-created bug is then added to the tester's bug report list, which is handed over to the programmers at the end of the day.

Hours involved: Typical forty-hour workweek, but can often turn into a sixty- to eighty-hour workweek during game production.
Work environment: Game testers work exclusively at the office in the testing area.
Salary: Starting salary around $33,000; more experienced testers can make $50,000 and up.

Educational Qualifications

Testing is a great entry-level position in the video game industry. In fact, the majority of all game designers working today got their start in the industry as testers. The only qualification necessary for becoming a tester is a love for video games and some experience with the technical aspect of building video games. A college degree is usually not required to become a tester, but having either a bachelor in arts with an English major or some sort of technology-related degree could be very helpful.

Skills Set

Because testers are often required to play the same video game on multiple platforms (different consoles, different types of PCs), it is important that they are familiar with the many different platforms available on the market.

Equally as important, a tester must be a good video game player. Testers are expected to have fast gaming reflexes and a familiarity with the different types of modern-day gameplay mechanics. If you've never played a first-person shooter, but you love role-playing games, being a tester might not be right for you. A tester must be comfortable with all types of modern video games and should possess above-average skills as a gamer.

Personal Traits

Being patient and meticulous are the two most important personal traits of a tester. A tester has got to be able to play the same video game and the same level over and over again, without losing focus or concentration on the task at hand: finding bugs.

Enthusiasm for gaming and people skills are important, too. The programmers, artists, and game designers around you are going to be working very hard on the game you're testing every day. It's important that you give them positive feedback as well as criticism. Be honest: tell them how you feel about their game. After all, most people who will be purchasing the game you're testing will be just like you—people who love video games.

How to Get Your Foot in the Door

Because most people think of testing as getting paid to play video games, there is no shortage of young men and women interested in becoming testers. Checking your favorite game developer's Web site for information or calling game developers directly and asking if they're hiring testers is the best way to find out about testing jobs in your area. Be aware that some companies refer to testing as QA, or quality assurance. Another great way to become a tester is to start as an intern at a video game production company and work your way up to a tester.

Marketing

The job of the marketing department (also known as PR, or public relations) is to get information about a video game out to the public and to get as many people as excited as possible about the game's release. The marketing department must figure out how to sell the game, what the game's hook is, and how to generate public interest.

Microsoft Chairman Bill Gates *(left)*, pictured here doing a little marketing for his Xbox 360 console, knows how to get people excited about his latest products.

The marketing department also designs and organizes the game's advertisement campaign. They will put together events or parties centered around the game. They will generally do anything within their means to generate as much buzz about the game as possible leading up to its release and to keep gamers buying once the game is on the shelves.

Hours involved: Typical forty-hour workweek, but can often turn into a sixty- to eighty-hour workweek during game production.
Work environment: Working in the office or coordinating publicity and PR events out in the field.

Salary: Starting salary around $60,000; more experienced marketers can make $80,000 and up.

Educational Qualifications

An education in public relations, media relations, or advertising is key for anyone interested in a career in video game marketing. Outside of education, experience in marketing and connections in the video game industry can go a long way in convincing a video game company that you're the right person to market their game.

Skills Set

An understanding of how the advertising world works, including all the different ways in which video games are marketed, is an important quality to have. It is the job of the marketing department to understand what makes a game worth purchasing. Whether it's the celebrity voicing the lead character, an advanced new graphics engine, or a well-known game designer launching his or her newest game, the person marketing the game must have an understanding of how video games work and what makes a game successful in today's market.

Personal Traits

You've got to love talking about video games and have a great passion for the game you're selling. The majority of a video game marketer's time is spent pitching the game to different retailers, advertisers, and gamers in the hopes of convincing them to take an interest in the game.

You've also got to have excellent people skills. A marketer's most important asset is his or her relationships with others in the video game industry. You've got to be an outgoing, friendly person who enjoys the art of conversation and salesmanship.

Events such as the Electronic Entertainment Expo (E3) are important opportunities for video game marketers to get the public excited about the products coming out in the upcoming years.

How to Get Your Foot in the Door

Having connections in the video game industry is important for anyone interested in a career in video game marketing. Therefore, the best way to get your foot in the door is to gain as much experience as possible in the industry. Start by finding a summer internship with a video game company or with a marketing/PR company that works in the video game industry. Attending video game conferences and trade shows such as E3 (Electronic Entertainment Expo) can be a great way to meet others who work in the video game industry.

CHAPTER 5

Cutting Edge Careers

Cutting Edge Careers

Cutting Edge Careers

The Future of Computer Gaming

The future of video games lies not only in advanced graphics technologies and powerful computer engines, but also in innovative gameplay and online community interaction. Gamers today are just as interested in original, exciting game designs as they are in the latest, most impressive graphics and franchise sequels.

Nearly all video games today are built with a multiplayer, online component. Game genres such as the massive multi-player online role-playing game (MMORPG) can only be played with others through a high-speed Internet connection. Video games can no longer be thought of as private, one-player adventures. Instead, the world of video games today can be

The popularity of *World of Warcraft*, today's most successful massive multi-player online role-playing game (MMORPG), is a strong indication of the genre's importance to the future of video games.

described as one where gamers from all over meet to have fun, compete, and make friends.

In fact, video games have become such a popular, global phenomenon that they can even be found outside of your local arcade or your home console or PC. The world of mobile gaming allows people to play video games on the go simply by downloading the latest titles to their mobile phones. Playing video games through your Internet Web browser without having to download any software at all, known as Web-based gaming, has a bright, exciting future in the video game industry as well.

With the industry growing exponentially every day and in new and exciting directions, now more than ever is the perfect time to be thinking about a career in computer gaming.

With players able to play the latest video games on their cell phones, home consoles, and home computers, the computer gaming industry is expanding in new ways every day.

How to Prepare for a Career in Computer Gaming

Every person working today in the video game industry started with a passion for video games. Becoming familiar with the different genres of video games, focusing your attention on what elements of the video game production process interest you, and envisioning the types of games you would like to one day create are all excellent ways to prepare for a career in computer gaming.

With more powerful technology and greater means of storing video game data comes more room to focus on story. After all, video games at their essence are interactive stories that allow a gamer to enter a world he or she wouldn't normally visit and to do things he or she wouldn't normally do. Reading books is an important way to learn the mechanics of storytelling and to find inspiration for stories of your own. What types of stories excite you? What types of stories do you think would lend themselves best to a video game?

Finally, by understanding the different people and the technologies involved in creating your favorite video games, you'll begin to see video games as more than just a disc you pop into your home console or a piece of software you download onto your computer. You'll see them as a creative industry in which you might be able to one day create the game of your dreams.

GLOSSARY

alpha testing In the production testing process of a video game, this is the first playable, near-complete version of the video game in development.

artificial intelligence (AI) The simulated intelligence of an artificial being, usually a computer or piece of software.

beta testing In the production testing process of a video game, this is the second, more polished version of a video game in development; often released to the public as a free download for further testing.

bugs Problems in the software code that cause a game to act differently than intended.

code The building blocks of software; the language typed by the programmer to communicate with the computer.

coin-op Coin-operated, usually refers to arcade video game machines that require coins in order to play.

console gaming system Video game-playing hardware designed for home use. Unlike a home computer, a gaming console usually serves no purpose outside of playing video game software intended for that particular console.

design document A collection of visual examples and descriptions of a video game in the preproduction phase of development.

external development A development team that works freelance and is hired by a production company to develop a specific title.

first person shooter (FPS) A video game genre played from a first-person perspective, wherein the player must usually shoot his or her way out of a level in order to proceed.

foley stage The recording studio where a foley artist creates sound effects on different surfaces and with different objects or instruments.

genre A category of an artistic medium, like video games, with its own particular style.

high definition (HD) Refers to a digital video signal that broadcasts or plays in 720 or 1,080 lines of resolution (rows of pixels). It works only on designated high-definition televisions.

internal development A development team that works exclusively for one production company.

licensed property A pre-existing franchise, brand name, character, or story that has been licensed to be a video game.

MIDI Musical instrument digital interface; a way of transferring data between musical instruments (usually a synthesizer) and computers.

MMORPG Massive multiplayer online role-playing game; an online video game that takes place in a persistent world (continues even when you're not playing) and involves a community of other gamers.

original IP (intellectual property) A brand-new, original video game idea centered around an original character, theme, or world.

pixel An abbreviation for "picture element"; pixels are small dots that make up a larger picture on a computer or television display.

platform game A video game genre in which players must jump, climb, swim, or run across obstacles and platforms in order to achieve an objective or complete a level.

portable console A hand-held gaming device such as the Nintendo Game Boy or the Sony PSP.

real-time strategy (RTS) A video game genre usually involving war-themed strategy. Similar to a board game, yet players do not take individual turns but are constantly taking actions in order to win.

role-playing game (RPG) A video game genre involving the leveling up and advancing of a main character in a large, often fantasy-themed, immersive gaming world.

software A program designed to interact with a computer, informing it how to behave and what to do. Software can be anything from a video game, to a word processing application, to a virus protector.

FOR MORE
INFORMATION

AIAS (Academy of Interactive Arts & Sciences)
32622 Calabasas Road, Suite 220
Calabasas, CA 91302
(818) 876-0826
Web site: http://www.interactive.org

ESA (Entertainment Software Association)
575 7th Street NW, Suite 300
Washington, DC 20004
(202) 223-2400
Web site: http://www.theesa.com

ESRB (Entertainment Software Rating Board)
317 Madison Avenue, 22nd Floor
New York, NY 10017
(212) 759-0700
Web site: http://www.esrb.com

IGDA (International Game Developers Association)
870 Market Street, Suite 1181
San Francisco, CA 94102-3002
(415) 738-2104
Web site: http://www.igda.org

TIGA (The Independent Game Developers Association)
Brighton Business Centre
95 Ditchling Road
Brighton BN1 4ST
England
Web site: http://www.tiga.org

Web Sites

Due to the changing nature of Internet links, Rosen Publishing has developed an online list of Web sites related to the subject of this book. This site is updated regularly. Please use this link to access the list:

http://www.rosenlinks.com/cec/coga

FOR FURTHER READING

Bates, Bob. *Game Design: The Art and Business of Creating Games* (Prima Tech's Game Development). Roseville, CA: Prima, 2002.

DeMaria, Rusel, and Johnny L. Wilson. *High Score! The Illustrated History of Electronic Games. 2nd ed*. New York, NY: McGraw-Hill Osborne Media, 2003.

Fullerton, Tracy, Christopher Swain, and Steven Hoffman. *Game Design Workshop: Designing, Prototyping, and Playtesting Games*. San Francisco, CA: CMP Books, 2004.

Gershenfeld, Alan, Mark Loparco, and Cecilia Barajas. *Game Plan: The Insider's Guide to Breaking in and Succeeding in the Computer and Video Game Business*. New York, NY: St. Martin's Griffin, 2003.

Kent, Stephen L. *The Ultimate History of Video Games: From* Pong *to* Pokemon—*The Story Behind the Craze That Touched Our Lives and Changed the World*. Roseville, CA: Prima, 2001.

Kusher, David. *Masters of* Doom*: How Two Guys Created an Empire and Transformed Pop Culture*. New York, NY: Random House, 2003.

Poole, Steven. *Trigger Happy: Video Games and the Entertainment Revolution*. New York, NY: Arcade Publishing, 2000.

BIBLIOGRAPHY

About.com. "Annual U.S. Video Game Sales." From the NPD Group. Retrieved May 2006 (http://retailindustry.about.com/od/ seg_toys/a/bl_npd012703.htm).

Adams, Ernest. *Break Into the Game Industry: How to Get a Job Making Video Games*. Emeryville, CA: McGraw-Hill Osborne Media, 2003.

Carless, Simon, ed. *Game Developer Presents: Game Career Guide, Fall 2005*. San Francisco, CA: CMP United Business Media, 2004.

CNNMoney.com. "Video Game Set Sales Record in 2005." Retrieved May 2006 (http://money.cnn.com/2006/01/13/technology/ personaltech/gamesales/index.htm).

Costik.com. "I Have No Words & I Must Design." Retrieved May 2006 (http://www.costik.com/nowords.html).

Crawford, Chris. *Chris Crawford on Game Design*. Indianapolis, IN: New Riders Games, 2003.

Herman, Leonard, Jer Horwitz, Steve Kent, and Skyler Miller. "The History of Video Games." Gamespot.com. Retrieved May 2006 (http://www.gamespot.com/gamespot/features/video/hov).

Saltzman, Mark. *Game Creation and Careers: Insider Secrets from Industry Experts*. Indianapolis, IN: New Riders Games, 2003.

TheESA.com. "Top 10 Industry Facts." Retrieved May 2006 (http:// www.theesa.com/facts/top_10_facts.php).

U.S. Department of Labor. "Computer Programmers." Retrieved May 2006 (http://www.bls.gov/oco/ocos110.htm).

INDEX

About the Author

Matthew Robinson, a novelist and screenwriter, lives in Hollywood, California. He has been writing about the video game industry for the past few years, following the industry for the past decade, and playing video games his entire life.

Photo Credits

Cover top © www.istockphoto.com/Martin Cerny; cover bottom © Paul Sakuma/AP/Wide World Photos; pp. 4–5 Bruce Rolff/Shutterstock.com; p. 5 © AP/Wide World Photos; pp. 7, 48–49, 53 © Robyn Beck/AFP/Getty Images; p. 10 © Gail Albert Halaban/Corbis; p. 12 © Joel Saget/AFP/Getty Images; p. 16 © Kathy Willens/AP/Wide World Photos; p. 18 © David Paul Morris/AP/Wide World Photos; p. 22 © Lenny Ignelzi/AP/Wide World Photos; p. 26 © Ric Feld/AP/Wide World Photos; p. 28 © Derimais Lionel/Corbis Sygma; p. 30 © Alberto Rodriguez/Berliner Studio/BEImages for Business Wire/Getty Images; pp. 32, 43 © Tom Wagner/Corbis SABA; p. 35 © TWPhoto/Corbis; pp. 36–37 © David Kohl/AP/Wide World Photos; p. 39 © age fotostock/SuperStock; p. 46 © Chris Goodenow/Reuters/Corbis; p. 52 © www.worldofwarcraft.com.

Editor: Wayne Anderson; Series Designer: Evelyn Horovicz
Photo Researcher: Hilary Arnold